BAD HOBBY

ALSO BY KATHY FAGAN

Sycamore
Lip
The Charm
MOVING & ST RAGE
The Raft

BAD HOBBY

poems

KATHY FAGAN

MILKWEED EDITIONS

Published 2022 by Milkweed Editions
Printed in Canada
Cover design by Tijqua Daiker
Cover art by Fritha Strand
22 23 24 25 26 5 4 3 2 1
First Edition

Library of Congress Cataloging-in-Publication Data

Names: Fagan, Kathy, author.
Title: Bad hobby : poems / Kathy Fagan.
Description: First Edition. | Minneapolis, Minnesota : Milkweed Editions,
    2022. | Summary: "Bad Hobby is a hard-earned meditation on questions
    about lineage, caregiving, loss, and poetry"-- Provided by publisher.
Identifiers: LCCN 2022005010 (print) | LCCN 2022005011 (ebook) |
    ISBN 9781571315458 (trade paperback) | ISBN 9781571317612 (ebook)
Subjects: LCGFT: Poetry.
Classification: LCC PS3556.A326 B33 2022 (print) | LCC PS3556.A326
    (ebook) | DDC 811/.54--dc23
LC record available at https://lccn.loc.gov/2022005010
LC ebook record available at https://lccn.loc.gov/2022005011

Milkweed Editions is committed to ecological stewardship. We strive
to align our book production practices with this principle, and to reduce
the impact of our operations in the environment. We are a member of the
Green Press Initiative, a nonprofit coalition of publishers, manufacturers,
and authors working to protect the world's endangered forests and conserve
natural resources. *Bad Hobby* was printed on acid-free 100% postconsumer-
waste paper by Friesens Corporation.

To Bobby

CONTENTS

I

2

When I was a child, and I imagined a future life with children, I always wound up at the thought that one day I would be an orphan. Part of me looked forward to this time, as though in the moment both my parents had died, I would become like a star in the sky, beautifully and profoundly alone. But if I had children, I would never be that shining thing, enveloped by a darkness, completely untouched.

—Sheila Heti, *Motherhood*

DEDICATED

The way I remember it,
I caught beauty
Like a flu,

Via handshake or high five
Or a thank-you-
For-your-service

Between the guys at the VA.
The one who lurched
Toward me, touching

Me, saying:
You like poetry,
More vision than question.

The one who said,
Overhearing me correct
My Korean conflict-era dad:

*Go easy, you won't have him
Long.* Or the one
Who said: *You watch*

Him like a hawk;
Just let him go.
In the molecular

Biology lab, each tank
Full of impossibly
Small fish bears

A sign that says: You are responsible
For your own deads.
Plural. Sure.

The older I get, the more
I am reminded of song
Dedications on the radio.

I called Cousin Brucie
To send out "I've Got You,
Babe" to my parents

On their wedding anniversary.
When he played them
"Gypsies, Tramps, and Thieves,"

Bob and Mary Anne
Were understandably confused,
But appreciative nonetheless.

I myself have
Had three partners
In my lifetime,

And what I still love best about
Two of them
Is how I never had to explain

That joke. There was all that
Time listening
To radio or TV,

TV turned internet.
I wish I could
Dedicate those spent hours

Now to my mom,
So she could come back awhile.
She wouldn't have to know

She was dead,
Like we didn't know then
How much time was passing.

I would play
With her hair like I used to,
And tell her stories until

She began to doze off
Like she used to,
Waking only to say:

I didn't ever know you
Loved me, Kath. You never
Wanted affection from us, Kath.

Just like she used to.
The wrong song, somehow
The right song, playing on and on,

Like a perfect virus.

FOREST

When I found the tick,
I forgot the rules I'd read:
with thumb and forefinger I severed its body from mine—
just wanting it out of me,
as I've heard people say of babies and cancers.
I felt a mix of tenderness and disgust
for it then, like the twin
streams of blood and water
rinsing down the drain.

That summer I used English only
to write poems and speak with my lover,
yet the French insisted on speaking English to me:
You visit forêt? asked the pharmacist
in charge of medical emergencies like mine.
I heard f-o-r-a-y. Foray in a forêt.
Non, I said, *jamais*.

Not far from there, pears grow
in bottles suspended from the trees
to make a potent digestif.
As long as the fruit remains submerged
in the liqueur, the pear keeps whole indefinitely.

When my mother locked me out—
I was two, and three . . . —
I'd go to our willow tree,
wrap myself in its whips,
stroke its many sharp eyebrows with my hands.

The pharmacist asked me to
remove my tights to see where
the tick had lodged,
not far from my crotch. Exposed
like that, I thought I should feel more
embarrassed than I did.

I used to believe
I had been preserved by something.
Now I think I am
the preserving spirit—with my leafy fragrance, sound of wings
in the canopy, blood
draining swiftly from the head
as I look up, neither host nor guest. Exile
speaking for one reason only,
and the reason is love.

STRAY

The lamb is bleating circles round the pasture.
He slipped from his enclosure like a soul—
through three fences!—and because he's still nursing,
his calls draw alarming response from the herd.

He won't come to me, though I want to help,
this one they call Freezer for his not-distant future,
this one of ginger wool the color and texture
of my dead grandfather's hair behind his Bible.

And lo, there will be joyful celebration
when the shepherd delivers the stray back to his flock,
the ewe's teats near to bursting at his return.

How nice the little handfuls of my own
mammal breasts have felt when I cup them,
buoyed up above their human flesh.

You think the space you occupy is large
and then— You think your one life precious—

ANIMAL PRUDENCE

Mice drink the rainwater before dying by
the poison we set in the cupboard for them.
They come for the birdseed, and winter
is so gray here the sight of a single cardinal
can keep us warm for days. We'll justify
anything—and by we, I mean I, and by
I, I mean we, with our man-is-the-only-
animal-who and our manifest destiny, killers
each of us by greater or lesser degrees.
Instead of a gun or knife in my pocket
there are two notes. Unwhich the//
dandelion, reads one. I don't know what
it means but cannot throw it away;
it is soft as cashmere. The other says:
coffee, chocolate, birdseed. I should be
extinct by now, except I can't make it
onto that list either. Like toothpicks
made of plain wood, some things are
increasingly hard to find. Even when he was
a young drunk going deaf from target practice,
my father preferred picking his teeth
to brushing them. My mother preferred
crying. They bought or rented places
on streets named Castle, Ring, Greystone—
as if we were heroes in a Celtic epic.
Our romanticism was earned, and leaned
toward the gothic, but lichen aimed
for names on gravestones far
lovelier than our own. It seemed to last

a long time, that long time ago, finches
pixelating the hurricane fences,
cars idling exhaust, dandelions bolting
from flower to weed to delicacy,
like me. Egyptians prepared their dead
for a difficult journey; living is more
—I was going to say, more difficult,
but just plain more will do, imprudent—
unlike art—always falling below or rising
above the Aristotelian mean. In France,
a common rural road sign reads:
Animal Prudence. Purely cautionary,
it has nothing to do with Aristotle,
but offers sound advice nonetheless.
These days, I caution my father more
than he ever cautioned me. He hears
his aural hallucinations better and shows
greater interest: sportscasters at ballgames,
revelers at the parties he insists on.
He's got all his own teeth, so toothpicks
must do the job. His pockets fill with them.
There are always half a dozen rattling
like desert bones in my dryer. I think
of the mason who chiseled his face
in the cathedral wall; he couldn't write
his name. The yellow bouquets I'd offer
my mother by the fistful also got their name
in France: dent de lion, meaning teeth of the lion.

COOPER'S HAWK

That afternoon, out running errands
on a road filled with others like me, the sky
bent a moment with a hawk and its prey.
I remembered her then, not at the sight of them—

the driver to my left saw, too: the flap and glide
a few feet above traffic, air made visible
between the wing feathers and the finest hairs
of the limp squirrel's fur—I remembered her

because she'd taught me their names. This one,
Cooper's hawk, raids the nests of birds and small
mammals in spring. Unlike others that bite
to kill, it squeezes prey to death in its grip;

they've been known to drown their catch,
preferring to use their beaks for eating, never
as a weapon. My tolerance for "Nature, red in tooth
and claw," rose as my estrogen fell. The wish

to die died with my hormones, and with all that
powering down, I could finally hear myself
not think. Held tight in the hawk's talons,
the squirrel looked already dead, or maybe

dazed as it rode the sky above me. It looked
like the wet ponytail my neighbor's child wore
that night. She'd been in some sort of trouble
and was crying. When her father came

after her, she tried to defend herself.
No words, he said. No words.
I don't want to hear you speak with your mouth.

FARM EVENING IN THE BLUE SMOKE

And though it was late, with a storm coming in,
our friends sat on the porch, smoking and drinking.
I went to my room, the laughter and talk loud
but oddly dear to me. I had a drowsy thought about
the flock in the dark—did human noises
scare them?—then worried when the storm began:
would they huddle in the small barn
with the strays and wren, could they
half sleep, as I did, to the sound of rain
sluicing down the corrugated rooftops
and the awed tones of humans, their faces
film reel in the lightning?
For my part, it was too late to feel anything
but safe among the prey.

AT THE CHAMPION AVENUE LOW-INCOME
SENIOR & CHILD CARE SERVICES CENTER

When I told them it must be like dropping your kid
off at school their first day, all my parent friends
nodded and smiled uncomfortably, meaning
what would I know. I won't be taking solace
in the many firsts ahead. Here among the gray,
spotted, and brown heads of the seniors,
their soft flesh and angles, their obedience as they
sit as uprightly as they are able at white, parallel
tables, nobody cries, and very few speak.
When I seat Dad beside her, one senior tells me
she's ninety-four, presenting one hand, four
fingers in the air, just as she might have ninety
years ago with a stranger like me, now long gone.

Dad never liked me to talk:
Lower your voice, he'd say. If I was louder:
Put on your boxing gloves. Or: *You'll catch
more flies with honey than vinegar,* as if some day
I'd need the flies. I stopped talking, started writing
instead. I work full-time and Dad wants to die,
so I dropped him at the Champion Avenue
Low-Income Senior & Child Care Services Center,
a newish building, municipal and nondescript,
in a neighborhood that's been razed and rebuilt so often
it's got no discernible character left. There was bingo,
men playing poker in a corner. Red sauce and cheese ·

on white bread pizza for lunch. Dad, a big talker,
was an instant hit, but refused to return. *What
is the name of that animal,* someone asked me.
Where is Philip, asked someone else, over and over.
As if firsts and lasts were one and the same.

ACCUWEATHER: REAL FEEL

As I made out, first, wing,
then fur, I half-hoped for a kitten
kind of squee; at worst, the sci-fi
seahorse kind. But what I stopped for
in the road was a squirrel's lost
battle with a red-tailed hawk.
Both looked straight at me
in the Venn diagram we made,
our intersection being
Nothing to be done.

We were warned it's a jungle
out there. In here, too—
though, more often, a petting zoo,
with its matted coats
and molars, a few dry pellets
stuck to your mittens after.
Some do better than to weather it.
Some are known to feather a nest
with it. My people were never good
at reaping benefit.
Euphemism, they understood.
When rain chokes the air
they call the day a soft one.
I'm here by sheer luck.
No one is coming after.
Real Feel: soft dawn in the meadow,
the pups unseen by the passerby, the bitch
gone days ago.

KEELSON

Like a cracked cup of milk, the swan leaks
white on the wet dock. It's hard to know
if this is normal. I'm worried, and ashamed
to be. "Sensitive," it was called by the family,
in the hushed tones of a fatal diagnosis.
My grandfather, also sensitive, was a "great
reader," they said, a crease in his cuffed pants,
fedora on his head in all weathers. He retired
early from the Coty factory, lungs clotted
with sweet-smelling powder. Our rounds
included the library, the church, the river,
and the shoe store, each equally holy,
he and the salesperson zealously attentive
to the room needed for my toes to grow.
As he aged, he drank less and talked more,
played Simon & Garfunkel's "Parsley,
Sage, Rosemary, and Thyme" on his Victrola,
cooled tea in a saucer, drew in his shaky
hand what looked like boats with crosses
inside. "Keelson," he wrote underneath,
"Use this as a keelson." He'd dreamed it,
he said, many times, God gave him the vision.
How could I understand? I never saw
my immigrant grandparents exchange a warm
word, not a touch, not a glance, but I worried
them, joined them in that worry. They
sent me to drama camp once to help me
"come out of my shell." The teacher said
I had the melancholy look of an Audrey

Hepburn, only less "buoyant." Teachers
used to say, when you misspelled a word,
"Look it up in the dictionary." How can you
look it up in the dictionary if you can't spell
it? Before the internet, nothing and no one could
ask you, "Do you mean SWAN LAKE?"
when you looked up SWAN LEAK. Now,
when a Swiss friend texts "Let's go for perch
in Morges," my heart leaps with the poetry of it,
like a fish on the line, like the invisible keelsons
bobbing toward the dock. Look it up: you can
listen to a French speaker pronounce *Morges*,
see Audrey Hepburn's Swiss home nearby,
memorize the French words for tea, yogurt,
and cherries, which I long to buy
at market each day, and which, every day
as I practice, tumble from my mouth like
body parts from a dump truck. How familiar,
how reassuring I envision the puzzled, pitying,
mildly disgusted looks of incomprehension on
the vendors' faces to be. Which is why I stopped
speaking in the first place, and would sooner
go hungry than ask to be understood.

DAHLIA

When sometimes my dead
ones visit me in dreams, I hear
but do not see them,
like the parakeet repeating
its name each morning beneath
the floral cover of its cage
in the warbled *R*s of
my grandmother's brogue.
My therapist says I learned
to take comfort in language
from an early age. Conversely,
I may have been sensitized
to verbal rather than visual
cues. Mostly my dead vocalize
my name, or pieces of it,
as if I were meant to
build from its syllables someone
who is without them now
and will someday no longer be
in need of a name. *Pretty
bird, Pretty bird.* A November
dahlia auto-filling the horizon
with its petals at sunrise.

FORESHORTENING

The man I'd hired cut the mower's engine, shouting
uphill to me he had to go pick up his son. *Lost his license.*

DUI. He's a Afghan vet with that post-partum stress depression.
Seen things you and I can't even phantom. I thought I could,

so waved him off as understanding people do and turned away.
Skype and middle age had made me wary of being

looked at from below. Zelda Fitzgerald drew everything
from that perspective, as if seated always in the orchestra,

or a child at the foot of a drawer at the morgue.
When the neurologist illuminated my father's brain

scan at the VA, I had to readjust my own perspective
to understand that we were viewing from below.

Through jawbone, nostrils, eye sockets, a series
of curtains parted to reveal, finally, his frontal lobes,

twin prosceniums so dark, nothing could be seen.

COGNITION

I'm here, riverbank—
wearing John Berryman's glasses
like everyone else.

I was thinking that evergreen
looked like a Leonardo, i.e., the umbrella
pines of Rome.

I was thinking of their soft
candles in spring that aim toward
the sun like birds each

morning, careening beyond the visual
mayhem of geranium
red. In that color

riot, it's a relief to see female
finches & cardinals bland as cartoon
balloons overhead,

pitted stone fruits, aging
uteruses, pantoums all: repeat, repeat,
done. You want something

you don't have? What is it
you have now? The sky swims into the river,
the skylights & windows;

traffic writes its notes in script
each night.
The MoCA test requires that one recall only

five words: Velvet. Face. Church. Daisy. Red.
Dad got none of them.
With or without my glasses,

not one is not a picture I will never see.

MY FATHER

raked leaves into stacks much taller than I
and let me leap into every one
like bursting the sun
into pieces: the scrape of his rake,
the way leaves cushioned and cut,
their old book smell. A word can't gild
the spangle of his ungloved hand,
either my laugh or his,
more than it already was—it was
what we understood of love
that brought me up in the tumult.

BAD HOBBY

From his pocket, my dad pulls
A roll of wooden toothpicks
Bound with a rubber band.

We're driving to the VA
To have his toenails trimmed,
As we do every three months,

"A standing appointment,"
I used to say to him,
But he no longer gets the joke,

Asking only why I can't
Do it myself. And why won't I?
I've catheterized him,

Twice, but can't bring myself
To tend his feet, so like mine,
Wide with high arches—

Ballerina feet, my mom
Called them, none of us dancers.
Now that he's lived with me

For almost as long as he lived
With her, I'm beginning
To look like Mom—pissed.

The podiatry techs are always good-
Natured, thanking Dad for his service,
Raising their voices when

I remind them he can't hear.
The big toenail on his left foot
Looks to be made of horse hoof.

They cut and file but never
Hurt him. Some vets smoke outside
The building, waiting on rides.

Don't ever smoke, Kath,
Dad says, *"it's a bad hobby,"*
Scrambling his words, forgetting

Our ages and both our pasts.
The toothpicks he saves and reuses,
Even when broken, he calls

A bad hobby. And the drinking
He once was well enough to do.
Vets here age out at Korea;

Most are Vietnam, Gulf, Iraq,
Afghanistan. Since
The suspension of the draft,

Only the poorest of us
Serve. Like sports, the art of war
Holds little interest for me,

Though both are everywhere on
Display and, in theory, I get it:
Offense, defense, spectacle,

Competition. The Renaissance
Painter, Uccello, was commissioned
By a nobleman to paint the famous

Triptych of the Battle of San Romano,
A skirmish really, between
City-states, fought by mercenaries.

More than the birds he was
Nicknamed after, he loved linear
Perspective, using mathematics

To create a three-dimensional
Effect. The work hangs
In three European countries now,

In keeping with its divisive history,
And is considered Uccello's
Masterpiece. Painted with egg

Tempera on poplar, it reminds me
Of the tarot, with its broken staves,
Like toothpicks, and sexy horses.

The gold leaf's intact
On the bridles, but the silver
Of the soldiers' armor has oxidized,

Darkening to ghostly shades.
My mother's hobby was painting,
Is how I know.

Uccello's daughter, a Carmelite
Nun, was described by Vasari
As "a daughter who knew how to

Draw." None of her work survives.
Hobby derives from a Latin
Diminutive for horse, from which

We get hobbyhorse, as in one man's
Sport, another man's war.
On the other hand, habit

Is defined as a sustained
Appearance or condition, from *habeo*,
Meaning "I have, hold, keep." Known,

In some cases, as hard to break
Or more useful broken:
A spirit, a promise, a horse.

2

EMPIRE

I went out looking
at Europe & all its stones
its diagonal churches & bronze
horses my shoes clattering like their
shoes my eyes as wild

If the heart is a cup
if coins are diamonds
well then we are
full & we are rich

Here
baked sometimes inside the cake
is a favor not a file
Here
sometimes cake is all we eat

How pretty the pedestrians inside
their full-face haloes of dog fur

How historical the sites
of brokenhearted jubilee

How will I choose between
Heaven & Sorry
when I own so much
of both already

FOUNTAIN

Dogwood white knuckle it through January, February, March:
what do your pockets want with those hard stars?

Commissioned in the nineteenth century for thirsty horses,
municipal fountains in Kansas City, where visitors and locals alike
are now invited to kill time, outnumber those of Rome.

We mark time in our own ways.
My dad photographs sunrise and the moon in its phases:
calls each of them sunset.

I live in fear I'll age like him: I think
the word persimmon at sunrise, and for half and quarter moons,
    paper crane.

At sixteen my best friend's son knew his mother was dying.
Her hands stroking the cat were perfect.
His hands, folding cranes out of rolling papers, matched hers perfectly.

We call all paper things ephemera,
but one thumb-sized bird has hung on my bulletin board for so long
its pin's rusted out.

He is motherless now, incarcerated.
I am motherless now, aging.

I waste my time in the nature store. The shells of the aggressively
     predatory
snails are so beautiful,
my impulse is to put them in my mouth,

their perfection owed to repeating patterns,
what mathematicians call self-similarity.

The cat blinks at sunrise from my belly, as the cat before her did
     and the cat before:
ribbons of cloud and blue.

When I shower, water sprays from my fingers like change for the
     poor box
or the unclenching fists of dogwood, unfolded origami,
cat iris, the star in the persimmon where the seeds once slept—

I said like, as in: like we kill time.
I mean metaphor, as when time kills us back.

THE RULE OF THREE

One of the first I learned was the trinity, three persons in one
God: father, son, and holy spirit, née ghost. Then I started writing
JMJ on all my homework and tests, for good luck, but also because

My ballpoint's blue ink looked pretty beside the paper's purple
Ink, like the inside of a clamshell when I teared up or squinted
From the smell. Sometimes the sheets were wet and curled like

Petals reeking of gin, which is why it was called spirit duplication,
After the nonflammable alcohol used in the process. Jesus, Mary,
And Joseph, is what the three initials meant. I'd draw a cross from

The descending caret of the M and think of Mary, the mother,
And of the other Mary, not, weeping at the limp feet of the crucified
Jesus. Where was Joseph, I wondered, but never asked. We seemed

To pity him a little, for reasons I couldn't name, like my father,
Who was both my father and a son, and soon to be the son of
His father's ghost. When my grandmother was dying, she asked

Her only child, my mother, to go with her. Mom waited decades
To obey, but she finally went. Together in one grave now, they are
Two Marys, maybe with the Jesus of their most solitary prayers,

Petals littering their one stone's four corners. Being motherless,
Like being childless, is both good and bad, I think,
And it is a third thing, too, that is neither of these.

HELVETICA

Rain crushes the crushed silk of the lake
upon which swan armadas ride.

That would be one way to put it.
Dickinson wrote, "Our lives are Swiss."

That would be another, in this country
that bears no saints, being reasonable and cool,

unlike my uniforms from school,
the fast food jobs, the single bridesmaid

stint I still wear like a habit
of mind, or a tatt to the wrong forever.

Men talk in cafes looking like the same man,
different weights and ages,

and children laugh and cry exactly
like the ones at home. There is so little

to say and so many ways to say it.
Bees radioactive in their boxes, boxes

surrounded by poppy-dotted meadow, meadow
surrounded by gate. What is it we wish

to capture, we experts of hedge
and fence? The agitated boy in the park

wore a helmet but rode no bike.
His caregiver handled him

roughly, shoving him to and from
the playground mat. Another handled him more

gently after, using her body and voice
to circle but not to touch him. Cloud

panicles loft along the horizon,
or what passes as horizon here;

the Alps never part for them, they *keep*
apart. Crow—extrovert, ambassador—

taps its beak against its perch each time
I look away. Which I do often, my eye

drawn to the lake in a smooth line to swans
moving coolly, whitely, uncannily like

the paddle boats modeled after them.
Because of the anatomy of their trachea,

the so-called mute swans are less
vocal than others. A busload of touring

nuns stops to admire them,
speaking in a language I cannot place.

Other worlds wake up, other worlds go
to sleep. A woman kidnapped years ago emerges

with an infant from a Nigerian forest.
Nineteen Yazidi girls are incinerated in a cage

by their captors in Mosul for saying *No.*
Did I imagine that our textbooks used the word

neutral and the word *humane*
interchangeably? Adverbs assist the action,

we almost certainly were taught, circling
on the lake that mirrors us precisely.

OMPHALOS

How many times the blood rush of truck, bus, & subway
        has passed below my window.
How often this body, meant to bend & breed—squat like
        my mother's, her mother's, & hers—has
paced instead, inside its head, gazing skyward for a noun or phrase to
        shatter the glass of our locked cars & save us,
original cloud
        that might break over all:

raccoon washing its hands like a surgeon in the birdbath,
girl at the drive-through deciding only 42% of humanity
        sucks, the rest of them hungry or high,
their wheels aglow like daisies, their wounds debrided, unbridled . . .

Jesus, Mary, & Joseph, I have blamed you for everything—
        the decades broken like your rosaries, our few family belongings
missing, glued or taped . . .

                    Back home, the air
is scented with Japanese lilac & catalpa's orchid blooms—
        colonized & colonizing:
your body made to carry mine
        dismantled, finally,
        in flame, to this,
of which I am but remnant, a speck
fished from a tear duct with your tongue.

Whose easy laugh is that I'm hearing now?
Whose loneliness, unbroken, goes rolling in the blood?

THE GHOST ON THE HANDLE

The houses here are named La Vague and Chantebrise
like places in a childhood daydream,

an actual lake filled with literal swans.
As a kid, I was most at home in the pages of a book,

a bee sliding the banisters of the blue
delphinium. Apollinaire called his books,

in the soft golden bindings of the period,
his blocks of butter. The sun here is like that,

palpably stacked, flaking off the wavelets,
filling the boats with yellow flowers, crowning

the heads of the young couple arguing, body and soul.
He calls her Pig, whore. Pig, whore,

while she sobs and keeps trying to touch him.
I didn't know it then, but when I was her

age we were called borough girls: a little too
fashion-forward, filthy-mouthed, and ready

to settle at seventeen. The older you get
the less surprised you think you can be,

but when the bus with its Sans Voyageurs sign roars by,
I think of my child who won't ever get born, ghost

in a sunhat, shoulders narrow and pinked. A swan,
ungainly out of water, slaps up the shore to preen

with its knobbed orange beak. Mallarmé wrote that
everything in the world exists in order to end up in a book.

A golden book. Death, is not this the sunshine?

PREDATOR SATIATION

The cicada, little clock of self-sacrifice,
true bug of Jesus,

emerges in multitudes
to the waiting mouths of predators

so that a few might survive
to procreate. And while I, too,

have heard my biological timepiece ticking,
shaved and spread my legs

for it, fragrant and freshly vaccinated,
my heart would beat as neither

mother nor martyr.
Woman is man's most successful

domesticated animal.
I am no exception, childless or child-free.

There's no escape
until, of course, there is—

but not as the machines we were.
Our wristwatches seize

the spike tooth every sixty seconds,
the gold eyelid closes

slowly, blades of sun
blaring off the lake at solstice.

ACCUWEATHER: EPISODES OF SUNSHINE

AccuWeather predicts "episodes of sunshine"—

No doubt it's streaming.

In one episode, sun backlights the roses and the rosemary.
In the next, it turns birdfeeders bright as lanterns.
In the third (I'm binge-watching now) mist withdraws
                                        slowly from the grass.

Such a long time since morning
                meant no nightmare, no bellyache, no sleeping
with sheets pulled tight round my neck in all weathers.

Yet I am still my own best
                vampire. No matter how many times you die,
there's always someone to take your place.

Just the check, please, I've said again and again,
Just the check. Then I get so much more.

THE SUPREME FAREWELL OF HANDKERCHIEFS

My first time in the sky, I flew with my grandmother.
She wore high heels.
She'd come from the old country by boat,
cleaned for a living, died
before retiring from a factory job. The stewardess,
also in heels, awarded me a set of metal wings,
pin glued on the back;
some passengers received fresh decks of playing cards.
It was just like the footage you see of flying
in the 60s, except it was my real life. I wasn't scared
but held her hand anyway because I liked to
as we rolled, shuddered, and climbed,
everyone and everything we loved below us: goodbye goodbye.
At first, clouds parted like cream,
then bitch-slapped our little plane good until
we'd all had time to consider,
some asking why, I imagine; some asking why not.

How many times now has it happened?
Holding hand after hand in the air
or pressing both my hands together thinking of theirs:
that one's bones, this one's thumbs, another's tremor,
their grace, skin, temperature, pressure.
Why not here, in sky that stays
sky, flying like the birds I cannot stop
writing into poems no matter how many
people say, Enough with the effing birds!
Actually only poets say that.
And we're lying because there's never enough for us.

A juvenile sparrow hopped to our threshold, considered
what it might find inside.
Don't worry, baby, I said, we're okay.
And with a sound like tiny cards being shuffled,
it lifted its body back up to the sky.

BIRDS ARE PUBLIC ANIMALS OF CAPITALISM

I hate to begin another poem
        with birds, but it's late
                April & they're everywhere,
                        the commonest of them
                especially, sparrows, circling
        madly to dinner & mate,
& today, a soft rainy
        Monday, one hour before
                sunset in the parking garage
                        there are more of them
                than the freshly hung
        flyers from Counseling:
FEELING HOPELESS?
        YOU MATTER! posted
                on every floor & elevator
                        because two students in
                two weeks have jumped to
        their deaths from the roof
deck—&, I confess, I like
        pattern, irony, & coincidence
                more than most, but I hate,
                        a little, the sparrows today,
                their industry & bad tempers,
        the instincts that keep them
alive, just as I hate my own
        language: the name of the last
                jumper from 16th century
                        Old English, meaning bird

blind, given to their hunters.
        Can't Counseling do better
than YOU MATTER?
        We *are* matter, maybe?
            We *are* hopeless?
                Emerson cultivated maize for many
            decades. A deep thinker,
        he believed we reap
what we sow. Yes & no.
        I wanted to die once;
            I can't say why I didn't,
                except that I desired,
            finally, more
        everything: food, love—
& sometimes got it. Did we ever
        have our names made fun of
            at school? Did we find there
                Saturn's rings through a telescope
            or spin the rings of an agate
        we held in our hands?
During Mao's "Great Leap
        Forward," his "Kill a Sparrow
            Campaign" eradicated 3 million
                birds. People drummed day & night
            until sparrows dropped dead,
        exhausted, out of the sky—
citizens shoveled dead
        birds onto trucks to clear
            the streets of them.
                The ensuing proliferation
            of locusts caused famine
        that killed 40 million Chinese.

Crop planes plow the air
　　　this morning, spraying
　　　　　for gypsy moth. Italy's new
　　　　　　　regime plans to register
　　　　　its Romani population; while
　　　here, we imprison children.
When planting a garden,
　　　intentions are mostly good.
　　　　　Sparrows eat some seed
　　　　　　　& crop, but only their share.
　　　　　We humans are greedier,
　　　wanting everything we see,
changing everything we touch,
　　　wanting to matter no matter
　　　　　how wingless & shattered
　　　　　　　the rings of our hearts.

PERSONAL ITEM

Even on his second circuit of the terminal,
my friend's brother doesn't recognize me
the day after her memorial service.

Who thinks to look for links to dead family
when at last you head home,
your only reason for ever being here

now gone? The second time
he walks by, I notice how much he looks
like her, and that his pants are too short,

just as they had been in the slideshow
of her life, when they were kids growing up
too fast for anyone but them

to mark the slow passage of time, the ill-fitting
and specific loneliness of children
we carry with us no matter where we go.

THE CHILDREN

Child in a Sandbox

I'd got his blue cap right,
& the blue of the leaves,
that it was the back of him I'd seen
squatting over bucket & pail,
the comma his ear made, frenulum at the center of his neck.

I got the coat wrong,
& added the unevenly worn heels of his shoes.
I'd exposed the skin between his pant hem & sock,
the socks without elastic left,

& made his back more aggressively curved
than is common for a boy. I'd turned
pale yellow light into gold—

& the pigeons guzzling
sand that was once, so long ago, the rock he'd kicked
past me on his way?

They, too, were my invention.

My Children

One's a little heart
palpitation
Nobody knows it but me

One's a willow
whip with its leaves shorn off
I call it Rosemary

One's a pirate princess priest
a Look at the horses or
toes curled under the diving board

Paisleys and hexagons each
has a point
to make

Heat
across my shoulder
just under the chin

When they say
we never asked to be born
they mean it sincerely

They mean Look
we are the horizon

How will you punish us now
How will you tuck us in

Childless

Some women are all the mother to all the baby.
All the tit out hip out flat of the hand & tone of
the voice. They never knew real love before nor
sacrifice nor strength. Enjoy them while they're
this age & sleep when they sleep are they sleeping
my youngest. I brought you into this world I can
take you out. All not in your bed not on their backs
or bellies either. Take thumbs out their mouths &
cats out their cribs. Some women run all the baby
bath water cook all the baby dinner list all the baby
rule night after night after they brought you into this
night why would they put you out. Their baby's snow
angels don't look like ours. They have juice boxes.
They don't stay down. When my wings close they
                                        close on nothing.

"WHERE I AM GOING"/"I DARE TO LIVE"

Lucille Clifton / Anne Sexton

I can't say grief lived there because nothing ever did.
Its purpose seemed to be to wait, and, like me,
to contain its waiting. When the priests
called Rachel, Sarah, and Elizabeth barren, I could
think only of cathedrals and railway stations, specifically dust
swirling in tunnels of light, the clockwork
sounds of wings and footsteps. When I studied
the ancient practice ostraka, I smashed an empty
flower pot, wrote my brother's name in magic marker on a shard,
exiled him from the empire. To my surprise,
he cried. I'd forgotten what it was I felt—I needed
to see. Outside had taken me
in. I loved it not
for its vastness but minutiae,
which I observed with the attention of one who is not herself
observed and cannot bear to be.
Mica in the pavement, larva in the rose. I fetishized
the sea monkey, diorama, created little worlds of
rules: if you see wind holes in the cedars
on one side, you miss sparrows nesting
on the other, and if you leave the utility lines out of your
picture, you're not being
honest. Be honest: when I first saw real wallflowers
spangle at the preserve in their tiny deer-proof cages, I became
breathless: to be singled out, protected—
We girls saved our cigarette ashes to fade our Levi's with.
We crisped our hair with curling wands.
We always smelled like smoke, playing
as we did with fire, like Bovary or Butterfly, without beauty

or the babies. One friend, a nurse now,
sent video of Johnny Depp on a pediatric oncology ward.
He visited, as Captain Jack Sparrow, one patient
in particular. Piracy and stardom
had never been easier: the girl leapt into his arms.
Her silent mother was more reluctant—
she knew how to wait.
As did those barren women of the Bible,
all of whose wombs were "opened" by God for acts of faith,
some giving birth well into their nineties.
Except for one.
Daughter of Saul, wife of David, who, failing them both, displeased
the Lord, and about whom it is written,
"Michal had no child to the day of her death."

TOPLESS

I saw my mother naked in the tub once,
but don't remember being naked in front of her.
It stands to reason I must have been, often,
though I was a shy child, and that's stuck,
blushing even now if I accidentally bare
the most virginal inch of cleavage. But
the summer I was nine I stripped
my shirt off like the boys, and everyone looked,
but no one said a thing—not even my mother—
until a well-developed neighbor girl told
me, kindly, that I should cover up.
With my round shoulders and child-sized
breasts, I thought I looked about the same
as a chubby boy. I know I sometimes felt
as strong as one. And as despised.
Too big to hide, too soft to be safe.

MINT

I asked my students did we still use the term
skirt chaser and they all said no, looking a little
sorry for me. No to coins in the parking meters,
which now accept credit, so no to hoarding
change in the hard plastic well near the hand
brake and god knows what. No to religious
statues for as long as anyone can remember, no
to magnets, yes to air fresheners, and yes to the new
bobbleheads, which are much like the old bobbleheads,
only less offensive. It's never all about change, is it?
Just mostly. Especially in poetry. Always a nickel
dulling in the powdered soap of those days, someone
seated in a webbed folding chair with a housecoat on,
there in the open door of the garage or breezeway,
the tenement, hospital, or candy store. Or there
on the stoop or stairs, on the porch, or in the window.
Still so many women in doorways and windows
the world over, their time as mothers or mothers
to no one long past, and having neither will nor strength
to pull up hose, zip a skirt, or button a blouse with
stiff fingers, they do not wave when you wave,
and why, in heaven's name, they might say, would they?
Women in housecoats, or housedresses, women
in scuff slippers, like school uniforms. Aging women
as the new tattoo. Which is why I could never have one.
What would I choose for this body, with its changing
skins, its tits and its hips and its two pink mouths,
its hands a threshold of so-often-idle and digging-for-
something, or waving and waving then closing the door.

MORNING

I walk out each morning, the sun on my back.
It is not the hand of my mother. She is dead now.
It is not the hand of my father. He is needy as a child
and cannot think to comfort me.
I won't say god, but you might.
Often in poems you means I and I means you,
and with our common griefs, confusions, and best efforts
unacknowledged, that may be true outside poems, too.
The sun feels good, it feels warm on my back.
The heat between my shoulders reminds me of something,
like the riddle beginning *what* and ending *everything*
that would love you and kill you but doesn't.

3

LATECOMER

When I discovered
Playlists last Christmas,
I made one for

My mother, dead
Three years. It was
Easy, I just backed all the way

Up under the tree
Lights and listened
To the background noise.

Sure, there was something
Of the clutch,
Glove, and handkerchief

About it, the sentimentality
I thought once
Might kill me.

But it was Christmas,
And missing her
Was all

That could hurt
Me now. Or
Half what would.

The other being
The memory of her
Body, which made me.

She was alone
When she died,
When she went

Cold, then rigid,
Then ash, the flesh
And bones that held me,

Fed me, pushed me
Out too far or in
Too close. The bones

From which the marrow
Was extracted, twice,
The bones she complained

She couldn't see
Beneath our chub.
Her skull I touched

Often beneath her
Curls, which I brushed
To a burnished glow,

Her scalp releasing
A few chestnut hairs—
So different from mine—

And the scent of
Soap and something
I thought of as grown–

Up woman. I stood
Behind her on the couch,
Straddling her shoulders

With my legs,
Her head at arm's reach,
Until she fell

Asleep there;
It must have been
The Valium

Prescribed for her
Depression and anxiety, neither
Called those then.

There are names
For everything now.
There are hearts

You can illuminate
For every song you wish to
Save. Memory

Is the only ghost.

WHAT KIND OF FOOL AM I

I'm not yet old enough to see everyone as the ghost of
someone else, but I'm old enough to do the math.

In 1962, Anthony Newley wrote and starred in the hit
musical, *Stop the World—I Want to Get Off.* Mom

played the soundtrack so loud and so often,
a neighbor left an anonymous note saying,

Stop the Record—Please Turn It Off. Years later,
when I heard Bowie's tremolo, I thought it

had to be Newley. Turns out, everyone copied him;
most are dead now. Mom taught me, by example,

the Murphy bed approach to housekeeping,
i.e, the appearance of order. Deep cleaning was

saved for another day, like our own feelings,
which were best bought, eaten, drunk, smacked,

fucked, or played on the turntable loud enough
to drown out the crying. My house is clean

and orderly both. I have learned to use
like against like for marks and stains—protein

for protein, oil for oil, unguent for unguent.
It is wrong to think that we are unlike others.

As a little girl, I could belt the refrain:
"Why can't I fall in love / like any other man?"

It is wrong to think that we are not. Newley
died playing Vegas. Spotlights looked smokier then,

bleaching what was lit in them, like our security
lights in rain, under which, when tripped,

one is unable to identify who you are, or what,
while all you see, at the edge of your world, is dark.

CONQUEROR

The lights are green as far as I can see
all down the street, sweet spot pre-dawn,
a Sunday, no one out. I measure time
in travel now. This route's a favorite, half
derelict, half grand, an oak hydrangea
blooming on old wood. I left a note
in felt tip for my dad, prepped him, then
reminded him last night, but at 4 I had to
mime and mouth for him *Go back to bed*,
my head tilted on sideways prayer hands.
He looked blank, obeyed. The ophthalmologist
explained how hard it is to see behind
his pupils; I forget the reasons why.
I'm at the terminal with the other early flyers,
thinking of the faces of the ancient kings
I've seen, their ears of stone, and their eyes,
no matter the direction or the time, looking,
as we must presume, ahead, and not inside.

SCHOOL

These days, just before dawn, I find myself
asking Mom if I can stay home from school.
I teach school now and Mom is dead, but
when I was a kid and said I didn't want to go,
she wouldn't make me. She'd pass a cool palm
over my forehead and get on with her day.
Sometimes we'd nap together, but mostly she
went to her job and I'd be alone all day.
I don't remember what I did, and she never
once asked me, never once asked why
I wanted to stay home, and so I didn't ask
myself. She must have trusted me, or not
much cared, which may be trust's result.
I stayed home because some days it felt
perilous to be seen, and other days it felt
perilous not to be, and these mornings it is
so much both that I do not tell my students
or family because I think they must trust me,
and because I think they don't much care
whether I'm alone all day with them or not.

ACCUWEATHER: WINDY, WITH CLOUDS BREAKING

My note from the night before reads
Drink water. Lots of water. Only water.

For when clouds break
                it matters they be empty.

The performance coach says *It matters*
you know how your look reads.

On another note
are the syllables *mots-a-rell-a*
so Dad will eat the cheese he no longer has the word for.

On another, *Mr. Goldstrike*, for the zone-appropriate plant
I can't remember the look of right now.

So much is about forgetting.

Wind scrubbing the young stands of sycamore at the river
until they reach like tuning forks. Clouds breaking
                as if we could see inside.

WINDOW

You know how it is with technology:
you pull what you thought you wanted
to print from the tray, a stack of somebody's
poems for your morning class,

& because you're in a hurry you toss
them in your backpack—like the napkins,
straws, & condiments you'd bag
for customers at the drive-through—knowing

how quaint the students will find handouts
of a poem they'd gladly read
on their phones, & because you reached humiliation
saturation level years ago, but far too late

to remember being ashamed by nothing,
you laugh—oh madcap, oh aging, oh absentminded
Professor Me!—when they see, as you pass
them out, that each sheet has printed

a thumbnail portrait of you in the left corner
followed, two inches down, by

a tree

ppiness

which of course is not the poem you'd wished for
them to have, & when, after the half-
hearted laughter dies down, you take
out your phone & they take out theirs

& you read the poem out loud
from the tiny screen (you would have said
aloud, back when you worked drive-through,
though you did not think yourself a snob),

your hand held far in front so you can see,
you feel the poem give, give
utterly; you feel the poem
taken & received, a light in every face.

TRACE

The pencil's pressure, lead both hard and soft,
so there and not, I questioned
the very physics of the thing,
as if I were lifting,
like files to a magnet,
the image from beneath the onion skin,
what my mother called tracing paper,
material light as a veil and stiff
as her bridal gown.
How could both continue to exist?

Once, I showed her something so
unlike my traces, I believed
she'd deem it genius: watercolor
on cling wrap, like a new
stained glass. I said
I planned to enter it
into the school art competition. I was eight.
She encouraged me, instead, to submit
art we'd made together,
her hand more evident than mine.

Not long before
she died, I mailed her a portable
watercolor set. I found it unopened
at her two-room apartment after.
I took it and the few things
that fit in my suitcase.
We were ashamed of each other

in ways only intimates can be.
They say you cannot love another
until you love yourself,
but I'm not sure that's true.
First, I loved my mother,
just as the one that drew and the one
that copied, by virtue of their separate
gazes loved, for as long as their attention
lasted, the original object
apart from them, whole only
for the duration of that gaze.

WISDOM

How often can you pass
a photo of your family
thinking,
These faces look familiar,
and not find yourself
ridiculous.

I sized the pricey
handmade paper I'd been
saving, the one
with gold detail, to mat
the picture, too old to fit
anything store-

bought; my mother
barely a teenager,
her mother maybe
thirty-five. I'd guess
they're in the Catskills,
a vacation

favorite in the 40s
with the Irish, a joke
in the 80s,
desirable again today.
For once
they look not-angry:

Nana proud,
Mom her beloved
and loving child.
In this they are and are not
themselves,
as I was

when they lived,
believing myself,
as children will,
the focus of their every
thought.
They fought

so long and hard
above me
I half-
expected Solomon
to wisely intervene;
if he ordered me

split, they'd have
to quit.
Not a single
photo of the three of us exists.

AFTERMATH

The VA nurse shows me how to dress
the wound of my father's biopsy at home,
my father who hasn't flinched through the cutting,
and though he hears close to nothing banters cheerfully at,
if not with, his fellow ex-Marine, who served two tours
as a medic in Iraq, back when he was married, he says,
and a father already himself.

              Something about having had to cut deeper.
Something about applying pressure
should the wound bleed excessively
and what that would look like.

    Ma'am?

I've studied his rubber shoes, wondered
if his ex-wife's remarried.

    Ma'am? Please tell your father—

What can I tell my father? How will I
tell it to him?

    —please tell your father how grateful we are for his service.

***

My mother and I, in a moment's shared vision,
see an angel in the mission,
and because I am the "parentified" child,
I am the one to investigate, finding
nothing out of the ordinary—
if you can call the neon pink of the bougainvillea ordinary,
and the cool walls of the church, built of mud, piss, and mule hair,
and the floating frankincense, dust, and sunlight of the air,
and all our colonizer ignorance and imagination, ordinary.

When I dream of her now, as I rarely do, we fly
Renaissance inventions side by side
with all the other animals. I never see
her face.

***

The wind and generational memory: the train and its trail of cloud:
    image and its aftermath:
the mind with its list of *like this not that*: patterns & parallels.

Math means first harvest; aftermath, a subsequent crop: what
    grows in mown pastures.

Look at the meadow inflected by wind where the mower hasn't
been. The mind with its list. The way it pushes down the grasses
like deer. And the remembered grasses. By remembered deer. Look
at them all bending where the mower hasn't been.

We switchback home like the train. Clouds shear off above, while,
at eye level, turning like wheel spokes, parallel rows lead green
words to the vanishing point.

***

Look at the meadow bending
      where the mower hasn't been,
      the petal fall on wind that sounds
like waves in the ocean Ohio remembers
      being. Now, as either wave or wind,
      it only wants us gone, or rather
takes no note of us at all
      except as objects to strike against
      to make a music.

***

Dad is singing me happy birthday.
It's not, I say, over and over, until he hears
and understands me, shakes his head in disbelief and says,
I guess I'll just have to accept that.

Meanwhile the wrens start up their own trills, full-throated
like ours, only a real discussion.
Do I sound bitter, I'd ask if I were joking.

True to his word, Dad's already moved on, singing
off-key to Christian programming, while I
kitchen-scissor salmon into edible portions.

***

And when he asks
for the thousandth time,
Who can I speak to
about this situation,
Kath, why can't I
answer, *Okay, Dad,*

we'll talk to someone.
I'll make an appointment
and we can talk to someone.

***

Bouquets of dandelions, fireflies, drawings, words
in books and songs and hurts to spare
like the weight of sun on the horizon.

***

Benign neglect is how my brother says we were raised. Free-range
kids, we say gamely about ourselves.

Our family name: a variation of pagan, one without envy, tall one
who fights dragons, one who is unnaturally pale.

***

In therapy we're working on "integrating my personality," which
would make T.S. Eliot spit. And because my parents lost their
"coalition" when I was very young, it's a challenge for me to know
who I am in relation to self and others. Okay.

But when I found the tiny gray toad on the toilet tank, I did what Mom would have wanted me to do: I saved it. I showed it to Dad, told him it felt like a tiny pachyderm in my hand, forgetting for a moment. *Better put it out in the pachysandra then, Kath—why do I know that word?*

MY MOTHER

is not a ghost. She doesn't visit or haunt me.
I'd like to dream of her but do not.

Instead she leaves me things: a string of green
Mardi Gras beads in the parking lot,

a goldtone Mizpah coin, a shiny mandala
freed of its earring. Things a magpie might pick

up, I pick up, knowing unquestionably
they are gifts from her, the alchemy all mine,

as if we were girls together at the mall,
festooning ourselves in jewelry, the kind that's 2

for 5, saying, *That looks so good on you!*
Our faces in such bright agreement

among the reflective metals, I
can no longer tell which one of us is alive.

OHIO SPRING

I mean, I had to
Play at least once, so I
Forced Dad into it,

Pretending I was interested
In his social life,
The Activity Center filled

With cliques of senior
Women, resembling
Cliques of junior women, plus

Dad, the Activities Director
& me, gleeful with spring,
Game & the chance

To laugh at my home
State. Rutherford B. Hayes
& deviled eggs were Dad's

Answers to every question,
Much like his every question
Involved the life

Expectancy of Canada
Geese, which bred on
The grounds, while cloud

Galaxies of redbud
Floated in the green
Of true spring outdoors.

There was no square on
The board for redbud, Canada
Geese or pothole, just as

There is no word for him
Now for "dead," for
"Room" or the sequence

Of his three daily meals.
I want to be, Dad says,
The next guy in

The cemetery. My mind,
He taps his forehead, *is*
Gone, a joke

No longer. If he lasts
Much longer, he'll be
Snowed with meds & tied

To a wheelchair. One
Has to wish instead
For the cemetery. Old goose

Drunk-stepping the lawn,
Gray-throated as an aged
Dog, there's nothing wrong

With you except
You're still here.
When I hug him

Goodbye, Dad says,
You're always in me,
Like it's a promise.

But by which the poet-
Teacher in me understands
The Marine-cop in him

To mean, I will be
The last to leave him.

SNOW MOON & THE DEMENTIA UNIT

Dad called again to see how his daughter Kathy's doing,
and when I tell him I'm doing fine, he asks,

So you've talked to her recently? What did she say?
and really, what could I say then

about the moon crowning and slipping back inside
a cloud, my body as full as the sky's bodies, bodies

that live off their own bounty, until their bounty's gone.
It's theorized that Earth's magnetic poles flip

over time, leaving it vulnerable to harmful sunlight,
accounting perhaps for the mass extinctions

of dinosaur and Neanderthal. *Dad,* I might say, *it could happen
again.* Sometimes I wonder if the carrot is behind us,

especially when I'm around rich people. A girl doing lunges
in lululemons up the hill reminds me of immigrant

ladies ascending church steps on their knees. A red
RESERVED on a real estate sign in the neighborhood I like

to drive through. Red text in the prayerbooks Dad reads aloud
like a champ: *Mercy!* I worry I might value silence

over people. That birds, with all their *bougie bougie*
and *breaker breaker*, are the best communicators.

That Bobcats and Caterpillars are neither. That I'm killing
my jade plants. Mom pawned her big jade teardrop

necklace in the 80s, right after Dad tried to off himself
lying behind a running car in the closed garage.

The car died first. What did I know of their despair and why
did I know so much of it? Breathing the air and being

the air. She'd say, *I don't want your advice, I just want you
to listen.* Each time I shower, I think of the inventors

of the waterboard torture, along with those who commit
and suffer it. For Dad, birds of the air

and birds of the water are one bird. All trees, one tree.
How long do they live, he keeps asking.

How is my daughter Kathy doing. And honestly, Joachim,
husband of Anne, father of Mary, mercy,

I cannot answer.

SCARLET EXPERIMENT

"Split the Lark - and you'll find the Music -"
Emily Dickinson

"Now I am become Death . . ."
J. Robert Oppenheimer, father of the
atomic bomb, quoting *Bhagavad Gita*

Like my country I prefer to forget
most things. Our series of rentals
in California, for instance, zoysia grass
blazing straight for the oleander
at fence line, beyond them holograms
of mountain ranges, the Santa Anas, for one,
sharing a name with the seasonal winds,
as my brother and father share theirs.
In memory, they battle tooth to horn,
fear rising from their bodies like dust.
Ranchers would sacrifice their bulls
for the popular bear bullfight
entertainments of the nineteenth century.
By 1924, all the grizzlies were dead.
They put one on the flag instead.

His first time visiting the dementia unit,
my brother points at a picture book,
prompting our father to name
streets and buildings of the city we were
born in. "Luxury condominiums now,"
Dad reads flawlessly, "270 Broadway was
the birthplace of the Manhattan Project."
After we bombed Hiroshima in 1945,

scientists predicted nothing would grow
there. The following year, oleander returned,
thriving despite the rise of human dead.
People love a comeback. Hiroshima was
named a City of Peace and World
Heritage Site. The nuclear family is
encouraged daily to create new
memories. You can make anything end.

LUCKY STAR

There was a day in December Dad once considered
his lucky day, but now he forgets which day it was.

There's a day each April I think of as lucky,
but now cannot remember why.

There have been actual lucky days almost
every season of our lives, I'm sure,

but I can't place them for you now,
nor the brand of luck they brought us.

If there is a difference anymore
between joy and relief, I confess it's been rare

enough for me to find, an abstraction, like god,
and, like god, embodied once, in several forms—

I could name them all for you today.
Instead I'll say, there are the stars you wish on

and the uninhabitable matter they truly are.
You can wish on any star, with or without a name,

though they say those called *first* and *shooting*
are luckiest—neither stars, technically speaking.

Not to speak is the thing to remember. A wish
must stay secret to be granted, which often takes so long

it grows obsolete. Like Dad and me, you might
forget it. Your life's complete, with or without it.

INACTIVE FAULT, WITH ECHOES

Rain won't fall, won't fall, and won't.
When I learned the word *virga*

I learned how full a cloud could be,
every word worth an extended visit,

visit meaning to both comfort and afflict.
Small fingers falling, not falling,

smaller even than curbside locust leaves.
I had a wife once, Dad says,

Whatever happened to your mother?
There's a fault near here

that hasn't moved in thirty years.
We are our own seismic shift.

Vertical lines on my fingers
could be my mother's. Leaves

don't change as much as crisp
in this weather. Catalpa twists in place.

We cause pain, and relief from pain.
The rain won't fall.

Whatever happened to your mother
was probably my fault, Dad says.

Remembering is dangerous, he says,
when I remind him.

My small fingers once recoiled
from amoebas pictured in the science book.

The breasts of the women at his facility
rest quietly on their bellies,

ghost bellies, their elbow- and earlobes.
I lost her somehow, Dad says.

The van there reads, Angels on Assignment.
Catalpa twists in place,

its many green ears follow a voice
as you leave.

Visit me. Visit me soon.
I want the earth to lose us first.

NOTES

The italicized line in "Cooper's Hawk" is from Tennyson's "In Memoriam."

"Cognition" refers to the Montreal Cognitive Assessment (MoCA) test, which attempts to screen for cognitive dysfunction.

"Empire" nods to a song by the Beatles in the penultimate stanza and ends with lines adapted from a poem by Sabrina Orah Mark.

"The Ghost on the Handle" is a title borrowed from a painting by Paul Klee. The poem ends with words from a book of erasures by artist Tom Phillips called *A Humument: A Treated Victorian Novel.*

"The Supreme Farewell of Handkerchiefs" is a title borrowed from a line in "Brise Marine" by Stéphane Mallarmé.

"Child in a Sandbox" from "The Children" is based on the painting by Pierre Bonnard.

"'Where I Am Going'/'I Dare to Live'" is indebted to both Lucille Clifton and Anne Sexton, from whose work the title arose.

"My Mother" is loosely based on some of the syntactical and emotional structures used by Cole Swensen in *Gravesend.*

For many other poems in this book, I have these dear ones to thank: Philip Grandinetti, Pablo Tanguay, Natalie Shapero, Marcus Jackson, Marlene Kocan, Pierre Florian, the A. Llors, Lyndon Emsley, Marinella Mazzanti, and Dimitrios Sakellariou.

Thanks also to the Chalmers P. Wylie VA Clinic in Columbus, Ohio, for their expert care, to The Villas at St. Therese, and to Cherry Blossom Memory Care for their profound kindness.

And for everything, in everything, all words and deeds: my parents and theirs.

*

In loving memory: Rudy Grandinetti, father of my heart.

ACKNOWLEDGMENTS

Deepest gratitude to the editors and staff of the following publications where poems from *Bad Hobby* first appeared, sometimes in different forms: Academy of American Poets *Poem-A-Day* ("At the Champion Avenue Low-Income Senior & Child Care Services Center" & "Animal Prudence"), *The Adroit Journal* ("'Where I Am Going'/'I Dare to Live'"), *The Bennington Review* ("AccuWeather: Real Feel" & "Morning"), *The Birmingham Poetry Review* ("The Supreme Farewell of Handkerchiefs"), *Blackbird* ("Forest," "Cooper's Hawk," "Trace," & "Lucky Star"), *Crazyhorse* ("Keelson"), *Enchanting Verses Literary Review* ("Aftermath"), *Everyday Poems* (rept. "My Children"), *Foglifter* ("Topless"), *Kenyon Review Online* ("Conqueror"), *Los Angeles Review* ("Farm Evening in the Blue Smoke" & "Stray"), *Memorious* ("What Kind of Fool Am I"), *Narrative* ("My Children" & "Childless"), *The Nation* ("The Ghost on the Handle"), *New England Review* ("Dahlia," "Wisdom" & "My Father"), *Ninth Letter* ("My Mother" & "Birds Are Public Animals of Capitalism"), *Numéro Cinq* ("AccuWeather: Windy, with Clouds Breaking," "Cognition," "Foreshortening," & "Empire"), *On The Seawall* ("Bad Hobby"), *Pleiades* ("Dedicated"), *Plume* ("Mint" & "Fountain"), *Poetry* ("The Rule of Three"), *Southern Indiana Review* ("Predator Satiation"), *Tin House* ("Helvetica" & "Omphalos"), *Tongue* ("AccuWeather: Episodes of Sunshine"), and *Waxwing* ("School" & "Window").

My thanks to Tracy K. Smith who chose "Conqueror" for inclusion in *Best American Poetry 2021*, and to the *2022 Pushcart Prize* editors for reprinting "Dedicated." "Omphalos" is included in the anthology *What Things Cost*, a book about work, published by University Press of Kentucky in 2023.

Thanks also to Firefly Farms for a glorious solitary week, and
to both the Ohio Arts Council and the Greater Columbus Arts
Council's Ray Hanley Award Committee for funding which aided
the completion of this book.

KATHY FAGAN is the author of *Sycamore*, a finalist for the Kingsley Tufts Award. She is also the author of four previous collections, including *Lip*; *The Charm*; *MOVING & ST RAGE*, winner of the Vassar Miller Prize; and *The Raft*, winner of the National Poetry Series. Fagan's work has appeared in venues such as the *New York Times Sunday Magazine*, *Poetry*, *The Nation*, the *New Republic*, *Best American Poetry*, and the *Academy of American Poets Poem-A-Day*. She has received a National Endowment for the Arts Fellowship and an Ingram Merrill Foundation Fellowship, and served as the Frost Place poet in residence. Fagan is cofounder of the MFA program at The Ohio State University, where she teaches poetry, and coedits the Wheeler Poetry Prize Book Series for *The Journal* and The Ohio State University Press.

milkweed
EDITIONS

Founded as a nonprofit organization in 1980, Milkweed Editions
is an independent publisher. Our mission is to identify, nurture
and publish transformative literature, and build an engaged
community around it.

Milkweed Editions is based in Bdé Óta Othúŋwe (Minneapolis)
within Mní Sota Makhóčhe, the traditional homeland of
the Dakhóta people. Residing here since time immemorial,
Dakhóta people still call Mní Sota Makhóčhe home, with four
federally recognized Dakhóta nations and many more Dakhóta
people residing in what is now the state of Minnesota. Due to
continued legacies of colonization, genocide, and forced removal,
generations of Dakhóta people remain disenfranchised from their
traditional homeland. Presently, Mní Sota Makhóčhe has become
a refuge and home for many Indigenous nations and peoples,
including seven federally recognized Ojibwe nations. We humbly
encourage our readers to reflect upon the historical legacies held
in the lands they occupy.

milkweed.org

Milkweed Editions, an independent nonprofit publisher, gratefully acknowledges sustaining support from our Board of Directors; the Alan B. Slifka Foundation and its president, Riva Ariella Ritvo-Slifka; the Amazon Literary Partnership; the Ballard Spahr Foundation; *Copper Nickel*; the McKnight Foundation; the National Endowment for the Arts; the National Poetry Series; the Target Foundation; and other generous contributions from foundations, corporations, and individuals. Also, this activity is made possible by the voters of Minnesota through a Minnesota State Arts Board Operating Support grant, thanks to a legislative appropriation from the arts and cultural heritage fund. For a full listing of Milkweed Editions supporters, please visit milkweed.org.